One Line Management

Easy to find reference quotes for the

"One in Charge"

Compiled by Morgan Rodgers

CreateSpace Publishing

Copyright © 2007 by Morgan Rodgers

Cover design by Shana Corbin

ISBN-10 1434844684

ISBN-13 978-1434844682

All rights reserved

Published and printed in the United States of America

Additional copies of "One Line Management" may be obtained at www.createspace.com/3338143

One Line Management

Table of Contents

Attitude	5
Commitment	17
Communication	29
Confidence	37
Crisis Management	45
Empowerment	55
Getting Started	65
Leadership	73
Motivation	89
Pat on the Back	103
Team Work	109

Chapter 1 - Attitude

It is our attitude toward life that will determine life's attitude towards us.

Jack B. Turner

The trick to eating crow is to pretend it tastes good.

William Safire

Whether you think you can or think you can't, you're right.

Henry Ford

Enthusiasm is to attitude what breathing is to life.

Keith D. Harrell

Nothing great was ever achieved without enthusiasm.

Ralph Waldo Emerson

Enthusiasm is the greatest asset in the world.

Henry Chestea

I never lost a game, I just ran out of time.

Vince Lombardi

A pessimist sees the difficulty in every opportunity; an optimist sees the opportunity in every difficulty.

Winston Churchill

To build a winning team, you must first of all develop a winning attitude.

Lou Holtz

If winning isn't everything, why do they keep score.

Vince Lombardi

It's not over until it's over.

Yogi Berra

A positive mental attitude combined with definiteness of purpose is the starting point of all worthwhile achievement.

Napoleon Hill

A friend of mine has a great attitude; when something doesn't go his way, instead of crying over spilt milk, he just milks another cow.

Alexander Lockhart

You can't always control the circumstances in life, but you can control your attitude toward those circumstances.

Alexander Lockhart

They are able because they think they are able.

Vergil

The control center of your life is your attitude.

Norman Cousins

Your expression is the most important thing you can wear.

Sid Ascher

There is no substitute for a positive attitude.

Christopher John

Hire me an attitude; I can fill in the rest of the details.

Dieter Tischer

Act as if what you do makes a difference.

William James

In order to succeed we must first believe that we can.

Michael Kordia

The minute you start talking about what you're going to do if you lose, you have lost.

George Shultz

The first and most important step toward success is the feeling that we can succeed.

Herm Albright

The greatest discovery of any generation is that a human being can alter his life by altering his attitude.

William James

Once you replace negative thoughts with positive ones, you'll start having positive results.

Willie Nelson

If you can walk, you can dance.

Zimbabwean Proverb

As long as you're going to think anyway – you might as well think BIG.

Donald Trump

Nothing makes a woman more beautiful than the belief she is beautiful.

Sophia Loren

It is our attitude at the beginning of a difficult undertaking which, more than anything else, will determine the outcome.

William James

Always bear in mind that your own resolution to succeed is more important than any other one thing.

Abraham Lincoln

What I do best is share my enthusiasm.

Bill Gates

Think to yourself, "I'm going to hit the ball," and you can.

Ty Cobb

Believe you can make a difference, and you will.

Bill Clinton

He is able who thinks he is able.

Buddha

My main focus is on my game.

Tiger Wood

To be a great champion, believe you're the best.

Muhammad Ali

We are what we believe we are.

Benjamin N. Cardozo

It is your attitude more than your aptitude that will determine your altitude.

Dr. Gary V. Carter

If you don't like something, change it. If you can't change it, change your attitude.

Maya Angelou

Examine what you believe to be impossible, then change your belief.

Dr. Wayne Dyer

A man can succeed at anything for which he has unlimited enthusiasm.

Charles M. Schwab

Life is 10% what you make it and 90% how you take it.

Irving Berlin

Sooner or later, those who win are those who think they can.

Richard Bach

Whenever you're in conflict with someone, there is one factor that can make the difference between damaging your relationship and deepening it. That factor is attitude.

Timothy Bentley

It's not the load that breaks you down, it's the way your carry it.

Lena Horne

This is the precept by which I have lived: Prepare for the worst; expect the best; and take what comes.

Robert E. Speer

One person with a belief is equal to a force of ninety-nine who have only interests.

John Stuart Mill

I've always believed no matter how many shots I miss, I'm going to make the next one.

Isiah Thomas

Many an optimist has become rich by buying out a pessimist.

Robert G. Allen

I have learned from experience that the greater part of our happiness or misery depends on our dispositions and not on our circumstances.

Martha Washington

The man who wants to do something will find a way; a man who doesn't will find an excuse.

Stephen Dolley, Jr.

A happy person is not a person in a certain set of circumstances, but rather a person with a certain set of attitudes.

Hugh Downs

You'll never be a hot dog if you think like a weenie.

Mike Stewart

Your biggest competitor is your own view of your future.

Watts Wacker & Jim Taylor

The last of the human freedoms – to choose one's attitude is any given set of circumstances, to choose one's own way.

Viktor Frankl

Nothing can stop a man with the right mental attitude from achieving his goal; nothing can help the man with the wrong mental attitude.

Thomas Jefferson

Greatness comes with recognizing that your potential is limited only by how you choose, how you use your freedom, how resolve you are – in short, by your attitude.

Peter Koestenbaum

Life is a great big canvas, and you should throw all the paint on it you can.

Danny Kaye

High expectations are the key to everything.

Sam Walton

I haven't failed; I've found 10,000 ways that don't work.

Ben Franklin

For success, attitude is equally as important as ability.

Harry F. Banks

Success is peace of mind that is a direct result of self-satisfaction in knowing you did your best to become the best you are capable of becoming.

John Wooden

There are winds that blow against us no matter where we go, but the baseball players look at that and say, "Maybe it will help the ball over the fence in left field."

Ben Sumner

Do not pray for easy lives. Pray to be stronger.

John F. Kennedy

Success is how high you bounce when you hit bottom.

General George Patton

If you think it's going to rain, it will.

Clint Eastwood

It takes no more time to see the good side of life than to see the bad.

Jimmy Buffett

Years may wrinkle the skin, but to give up enthusiasm wrinkles the soul.

Samuel Ullman

I discovered I always have choices and sometimes it's only a choice of attitude.

Judith M. Knowlton

Success is a state of mind.

Joyce Brothers

My attitude is the only one I can control, but not the only one I affect.

Morgan Rodgers

Let's roll.

President George W. Bush

Chapter 2 – Commitment

If you aren't going all the way, why go at all.

Joe Namath

Nothing is interesting if you are not interested.

Helen Mac Inness

I have fought a good fight; I have finished my course; I have kept the faith.

II Timothy 4:7

It's not over until it's over.

Yogi Berra

Character consists of what you do on the third and fourth tries.

James Michener

My motto was always to keep swinging.

Hank Aaron

Frustration is commonly the difference between what you would like to be and what you are willing to sacrifice to become what you would like to be.

Sydney J. Harris

The way I see it, if you want the rainbow, you gotta put up with the rain.

Dolly Parton

Give the best that you have to the highest you know and do it now.

Ralph M. Sockman

The very first step towards success in any occupation is to become interested in it.

Sir William Oscar

When the race has started, there is no sense looking back.

Keith D. Harrell

Nothing in the world can take the place of persistence.

Calvin Coolidge

To be successful, the first thing to do is fall in love with your work.

Mary Lauretta

You must get involved to have an impact.

John H. Holcomb

It's not what you do once in a while; it's what you do day in and day out that makes a difference.

Jenny Craig

If I had eight hours to chop down a tree, I'd spend six hours sharpening my axe.

Abraham Lincoln

If someone had told me I would be Pope one day, I would have studied harder.

Pope John I

Even if I knew that tomorrow the world would go to pieces, I would still plant my apple tree.

Martin Luther

Let us have faith that right makes right, and in that faith let us to the end dare to do our duty as we understand it.

Abraham Lincoln

Do your work with your whole heart and you will succeed – there's so little competition.

Elbert Hubbard

Success seems to be largely a matter of hanging on after others have let go.

William Feather

All things are possible to him that believeth.

Mark 9:23

If you cannot win, make the one ahead of you break the record.

Jan McKeithen

One thought driven home is better than three left on base.

James Liter

It's always too early to quit.

Norman Vincent Peale

We must not only give what we have but also give what we are.

Cardinal Mercia

We can do anything we want to if we stick to it long enough.

Helen Keller

To climb steep hills requires slow pace at first.

William Shakespeare

Learn the fundamentals of the game and stick to them.

Jack Nicklaus

The secret to success is constancy of purpose.

Benjamin Disraeli

Decide what you want to be – pay the price.

John. A Widtsoe

Consider the postage stamp. It secures success through its ability to stick to one thing till it gets there.

Josh Billings

The slogan "press on" has solved and always will solve the problems of the human race.

Calvin Coolidge

After making a mistake or suffering a misfortune, the man of genius always gets back on his feet.

Napoleon Bonaparte

The most certain way to succeed is always to try just one more time.

Thomas Alva Edison

Victory – a matter of staying power.

Elbert G. Hubbard

I believe when you are in any contest you should work like there is –to the very last minute—a chance to lose it.

Dwight D. Eisenhower

Commitment is doing what you said you would do after the feeling you said it in has passed.

St. Camillus de Lellis

If you got the guts to stick it out, you are going to make it.

Brian Hays

Playing in the big leagues wasn't nearly as hard as getting there.

Hank Aaron

This one step – choosing a goal and sticking to it – changes everything.

Scott Reed

He conquers who endures.

Persius

Diamonds are nothing more than chucks of coal that stuck to their jobs.

Malcolm Stevenson Forbes

The majority of men meet with failure because of their lack of persistence in creating new plans to take the place of those which fail.

Napoleon Hill

Invest yourself in everything you do.

Wynton Marsalis

If you only knock long enough and loud enough at the gates, you are sure to wake up somebody.

Henry Wadsworth Longfellow

You've got to say, "I think that if I keep working at this and want it badly enough I can have it."

Lee J. Iacocca

We must never be too busy to take time to sharpen the saw.

Stephen R. Covey

The quality of a person's life is in direct proportion to their commitment to excellence, regardless of their chosen field.

Vince Lombardi

Always bear in mind that your own resolution to success is more important than any other one thing.

Abraham Lincoln

Everybody gets better if they keep at it.

Ted Williams

You can lose the first 14 rounds but you deck your opponent in the 15th round, you're champion of the world.

Ross Perot

Let us run with perseverance the race that is set before us.

Ecclesiastes 7:8

Never, never, never, never give up.

Winston Churchill

There is only one way to succeed in anything, and this is to give it everything.

Vince Lombardi

The achievement of your goals is assured the moment you commit yourself to it.

Mark R. Douglas

Why go into something to test the waters? (Go into it to make waves.)

Michael Nolan

Great works are performed not by strengths but by perseverance.

Samuel Jackson

We need to learn to set our course by the stars, not by the lights of every passing ship.

General Omar N. Bradley

Success consists of getting up just one more time than you fall.

Oliver Goldsmith

What we steadily, consciously, habitually think we are, that we tend to become.

Ann Landers

When defeat comes, accept it as a signal that your plans are not sound, rebuild those plans, and set sail once more toward your coveted goal.

Napoleon Hill

Competing in sports has taught me that if I'm not willing to give 120 percent, someone else will.

Ron Blomberg

Most of the important things in the world have been accomplished by people who have kept trying when there seemed to be no hope at all.

Dale Carnegie

If you don't invest very much, the defeat doesn't hurt much and winning is not very exciting.

Dick Vermeil

Never let a day pass that you will have cause to say, "I will do better tomorrow."

Brigham Young

In the confrontation between the stream and the rock, the stream always wins – not through strength, but by perseverance.

H. Jackson Brown

Chapter 3 – Communication

The genius of communication is the ability to be both totally honest and totally kind at the same time.

John Powell

A problem well stated is a problem half solved.

Charles Kettering

Few sinners are saved after the first 20 minutes of a sermon.

Mark Twain

Brevity is very good when we are, or are not, understood.

Samuel Butler

The more you say, the less people remember.

Francois Fenelow

The first key to networking is to talk to everyone.

Ken Blanchard

How well we communicate is determined not by how well we say things but how well we are understood.

Andrew Grove

If you don't give people information, they'll make up something to fill the void.

Carla O'Dell

Unless you truly want to understand the other person, you'll never be able to listen.

Mark Herndon

We rule the world by our words.

Napoleon Bonaparte

I wish people who have trouble communicating would just shut up.

Tom Lehrer

Many attempts to communicate are nullified by saying too much.

Robert Greenleaf

As a general rule, the most successful man in life is the man who has the best information.

Benjamin Disraeli

You cannot train a horse with shouts and expect it to obey a whisper.

Pagobert P. River

Everybody needs somebody that they can talk to.

John Prine

The most important thing in communication is to hear what isn't being said.

Peter F. Drucker

A loud voice cannot compete with a clear voice, even if it's a whisper.

Barry Neil Kaufman

A well informed employee is the best salesperson a company can have.

Edwin J. Thomas

They may forget what you said – but they will never forget how you made them feel.

Carl W. Buehner

The happiest conversation is where there is no competition, no vanity, but a clam quiet interchange of sentiments.

Samuel Johnson

The two words information and communication are often used interchangeably, but they signify quite different things. Information is going out; communication is getting through.

Sidney Harris

The great enemy of clear language is insincerity.

George Orwell

Seek first to understand, then to be understood.

Steven Covey

It takes a great man to be a good listener.

Calvin Coolidge

Speak when you are angry and you will make the best speech you will ever regret.

Ambrose Bierce

Most people do not listen with the intent to understand; they listen with the intent of reply.

Stephen Covey

People generally see what they look for and hear what they listen for.

Harper Lee

Speak softly and carry a big stick; you will go far.

Theodore Roosevelt

We need to listen to one another.

Chaim Potok

One advantage of talking to yourself is that you know at least somebody's listening.

Franklin P. Jones

Conversation means being able to disagree and still continue the conversation.

Dwight MacDonald

Every time you open your mouth you let men look into your mind.

Bruce Burton

Two monologues do not make a dialogue.

Jeff Daly

The art of communication is the language of leadership.

James Humes

Listening well is a powerful means of communication and influence.

John Marshall

Learn to listen. (Opportunity could be knocking at your door very softly.)

Frank Tyger

Hear the meaning within the word.

William Shakespeare

When the communicatee does not understand what the communicator intended, the responsibility remains that of the communicator.

Joe Batten

Each person's life is lived as a series of conversations.

Deborah Fannen

In conversation, keep in mind that you're more interested in what you have to say than anyone else is.

Andy Rooney

You can discover more about a person in an hour of play than in a year of conversation.

Plato

The less you talk, the more you're listened to.

Abigail Van Buren

There is always hope when people are forced to listen to both sides.

John Stuart Mill

To disagree, one doesn't have to be disagreeable.

Barry M. Goldwater

The music is nothing if the audience is deaf.

Walter Lippman

An individual without information cannot take responsibility; an individual who is given information cannot help but take responsibility.

Jan Carlson

As I get older, I've learned to listen to people rather than accuse them of things.

Po Bronson

Chapter 4 – Confidence

Remember no one can make you feel inferior without your consent.

Eleanor Roosevelt

In the game of life, as in other sports, you can pick out the winners – they're the ones who aren't complaining about the officiating.

Bill Vaughn

What we need are more people who specialize in the impossible.

Theodore Roosevelt

The ablest man I ever met is the man you think you are.

Franklin D. Roosevelt

Trust yourself. You know more than you think you do.

Benjamin Spock

I leave this rule for others when I'm dead -- be always sure you're right, then go ahead.

David Crockett

Making decisions is what leaders are paid for.

Joe D. Batten

Never tell me the odds.

Han Solo

Be so good they can't ignore you.

Jerry Dunn

Man cannot discover new oceans unless he has the courage to lose sight of the shore.

Andre Gide

Nothing is more powerful than an idea whose time has come.

Victor Hugo

Give your dreams all you've got and you'll be amazed at the energy that comes out of you.

Williams Jones

Self-confidence is the first requisite for any understanding.

Samuel Johnson

Confidence, like art, never comes from having all the answers; it comes from being open to all the questions.

Earl Stevens

Life consists not in holding good cards, but in playing those you hold well.

Josh Billings

Use what talents you possess; the woods would be silent if no birds sang except those that sing best.

Henry Van Dyke

Courage is being scared to death and saddling up anyway.

John Wayne

In order to succeed, you must know what you are doing, like what you are doing, and believe in what you are doing.

Anna Freud

You have to believe in yourself when no one else does – that makes you a winner right there.

Venus Williams

Experience tells you what to do; confidence allows you to do it.

Stan Smith

With confidence, you can reach truly amazing heights; without confidence, even the simplest accomplishments are beyond your grasp.

Jim Loehr

Winning breeds confidence and confidence breeds winning.

Hubert Green

I never hit a shot, not even in practice, without having a very sharp in focus picture of it in my mind.

Jack Nicklaus

If one advances confidently in the direction of his dreams, and endeavors to live the life which he has imagined, he will meet with a success unexpected in common hours.

Henry David Thoreau

I go into every game thinking I'm going to be the hero.

Derek Jeter

Confidence is contagious. (So is a lack of confidence.)

Michael O'Brien

We are not interested in the possibilities of defeat.

Queen Victoria

I was always looking outside myself for strength and confidence but it comes from within.

Anna Freud

You've got to take the initiative and play your game…confidence makes the difference.

Chris Evert

Never let the fear of striking out get in your way.

Babe Ruth

When we are confident, all we need is a little support.

Andre Laurendeau

I skate to where I think the puck will be.

Wayne Gretzky

Fortune favors the prepared mind.

Louis Pasteur

As in our confidence, so is our capacity.

William Huzlitt

Trust your gut.

Barbara Walters

Trust in your own untried capacity.

Ella Wheeler Wilcox

Besides pride, loyalty, discipline, heart and mind, confidence is the key to all the locks.

Joe Paterno

Change your thoughts and you change your world.

Norman Vincent Peale

If we did the things we are capable of doing, we would astound ourselves.

Thomas A. Edison

Go confidently in the direction of your dreams.

Henry David Thoreau

Faith is building on what you know is here, so you can reach what you know is there.

Cullen Hightower

You are what you think you are all day long.

Ralph Waldo Emerson

Nothing can dim the light which shines from within.

Maya Angelou

You are the one who can stretch your own horizon.

Edgar F. Magnin

If ye have faith…nothing shall be impossible unto you.

Matthew 17:20

Chapter 5 – Crisis Management

Courage is the art of being the only one who knows you're scared to death.

Earl Wilson

A problem is a chance for you to do your best.

Duke Ellington

Things turn out best for the people who make the best of the way things turn out.

Art Linkletter

People in distress will sometimes prefer a problem that is familiar to a solution that is not.

Neil Postman

Anyone can steer the ship when the sea is calm.

Publilius Syrus

Challenges make you discover things about yourself that you never really knew.

Cecily Tyson

Nothing gives one person so much advantage over another as to remain always cool and unruffled under all circumstances.

Thomas Jefferson

It doesn't matter what temperature the room is, it's always room temperature.

Steven Wright

You may not be able to control the situation, but you can always control your reaction.

Austin McGonigle

The only security we have is in our ability to fly by the seat of our pants.

Brad Blanton

You better start swimming or you'll sink like a stone.

Bob Dylan

The best way to escape from a problem is to solve it.

Alan Saporta

If you got the guts to stick it out, you are going to make it.

Brian Hays

The ultimate measure of a man is not where he stands in moments of comfort, but where he stands at times of challenge and controversy.

Martin Luther King, Jr.

Whatever the struggle, continue to climb, it may be only one step to the summit.

Dianne Westlake

He that will not sail till all dangers are over must never put to sea.

Thomas Fuller

In the middle of difficulty lies opportunity.

Albert Einstein

Only if you've been in the deepest valley can you ever know how magnificent it is to be on the highest mountain.

Richard M. Nixon

It's a little like wrestling a gorilla. You don't quit when you're tired – you quit when the gorilla gets tired.

Robert Strauss

If you're going through hell, keep going.

Winston Churchill

When written in Chinese, the word "crisis" is composed of two characters – one represents danger, and the other represents opportunity.

John F. Kennedy

The best way out is always through.

Robert Frost

The stronger the wind, the stronger the trees.

William Marriott

Whenever you see darkness, there is extraordinary opportunity for the light to burn brighter.

Bono

We must never become so busy slapping at mosquitoes that we walk into the quicksand.

Robert L. Evans

A time of disarray is also a moment of opportunity.

Frederick Ferre

The harder the conflict, the more glorious the triumph.

Thomas Paine

A pessimist sees the difficulty in every opportunity; an optimist sees the opportunity in every difficulty.

Winston Churchill

I think the next best thing to solving a problem is finding some humor in it.

Frank A. Clark

The greater the difficulty, the greater the glory.

Cicero

What does not destroy me makes me stronger.

Friedrich Nietzsche

The only safe ship in a storm is leadership.

Faye Wattleton

Don't give up at half time.

Bear Bryant

Without a struggle, there can be no progress.

Frederick Douglass

Problems are only opportunities in work clothes.

Henry Kaiser

The greater the difficulty, the more the glory in surmounting it.

Epicurus

Challenges are what make life interesting; overcoming them is what makes life meaningful.

Albert Einstein

The road to success is always under construction.

Lily Tomlin

Take arms against a sea of troubles; and in so doing, end them.

Shakespeare

In the midst of movement and chaos, keep stillness inside of you.

Deepak Chopra

The measure of a man is the way he bears up under misfortune.

Plutarch

Expect trouble as an inevitable part of life and repeat to yourself, the most comforting words of all: "This too shall pass."

Ann Landers

You learn more from ten days of agony than from ten years of content.

Sally Jessy Raphael

It is our duty to make the best of our misfortunes.

George Washington

If we had no winter, the spring would not be so pleasant.

Anne Bradstreet

When you get into a tight place and its seems you can't go on, hold on, for that's just the place and the time that the tide will turn.

Harriet Beecher Stowe

The hallmark of a well-managed organization is not the absence of problems, but whether or not problems are effectively resolved.

Steve Ventura

It's when you run away that you're most liable to stumble.

Casey Robinson

Opportunity's favorite disguise is trouble.

Frank Tyger

One of the secrets of life is to make stepping stones out of stumbling blocks.

Jack Penn

If you find yourself in a hole, the first thing to do is stop digging.

Mark Aaron

It has been my philosophy of life that difficulties vanish when faced boldly.

Isaac Asimov

There is in the worst of fortune the best of chances for a happy change.

Euripides

There are two ways of meeting difficulties: you alter the difficulties or you alter yourself meeting them.

Phyllis Bottome

When you can't solve the problem, manage it.

Rev. Robert H. Schuler

The darkest hour has only 60 minutes.

Morris Mandel

Storms make trees take deeper roots.

Claude McDonald

I'm not afraid of storms, for I'm learning how to sail my ship.

Louisa May Alcott

A good scare is worth more to man than good advice.

Edgar Watson Howe

Change before you have to.

Jack Welch

I always tried to turn every disaster into an opportunity.

John D. Rockefeller

Chapter 6 – Empowerment

What great thing would you attempt if you knew you could not fail?

Robert H. Schuler

A ship in a safe harbor is safe – that is not what a ship is built for.

William Shed

Treat people as if they were what they ought to be and you help them to become what they are capable of being.

Johann Von Goethe

You are not in charge of the universe; you are in charge of yourself.

Arnold Bennett

If you think you're too small to make a difference, you've never been in bed with a mosquito.

Anita Roddick

The more you do, the more you are.

Angie Papadakis

Opportunity dances with those already on the dance floor.

H. Jackson Brown

You can't learn anything from experiences you're not having.

Louis L'Amour

As our circumstances are new, we must think anew, and act anew.

Abraham Lincoln

If the 20th Century taught us anything, it is to be cautious about the word impossible.

Charles Platt

You have to be willing to step out of the pack and take risks, even jump completely out of your element if that's what it takes.

Carol Bartz

The answer is out there if you will look for it.

Thomas Edison

The time is always right to do what is right.

Martin Luther King, Jr.

"Do" is the critical word.

Peter Drucker

Don't be afraid to take one large step because you can't cross a chasm in two small leaps.

Lloyd George

Use what talent you possess; the woods would be silent if no birds sang except those that sang best.

Henry Van Dyke

It's better to be boldly decisive and risk being wrong than to agonize at length and be right too late.

Marilyn Moats Kennedy

Your destiny is in your hands, and your important decisions are your own to make.

Spencer K. Kimball

You miss 100% of the shots you never take.

Wayne Gretzky

Live the life you've imagined.

Thoreau

Life is a great big canvas, and you should throw all the paint on it you can.

Danny Kay

Things happen only when somebody makes them happen.

Manoj Kakkar

The smallest good deed is better than the grandest good intention.

Duguet

Fill what's empty; empty what's full; and scratch where it itches.

Duchess of Windsor

When you come to a fork in the road, take it.

Yogi Berra

You cannot make progress without making decisions.

Jim Rohn

Only those who risk going too far can possibly find out how far one can go.

T. S. Eliot

Hit the ball over the fence and you can take your time going around the bases.

John Rayser

We must sail sometimes with the wind and sometimes against it, but sail we must and not drift, nor lie in anchor

Oliver Wendell Holmes.

Do your job brilliantly and the cream will rise to the top.

Irene Rosenfeld

Whatever you are, be a good one.

Abraham Lincoln

Do what you can, with what you have, where you are.

Theodore Roosevelt

Whatever your life's work is, do it well.

Martin Luther King, Jr.

I'm not a good shot, but I shoot often.

Theodore Roosevelt

I am a slow walker, but I never walk backwards.

Abraham Lincoln

Change your thoughts and you change your world.

Norman Vincent Peale

If it's a good idea – go ahead and do it.

Grace Murry Hopper

Most of us are tiptoeing through life so we can reach death safely.

Tony Campolo

Go confidently in the direction of your dreams.

Henry David Thoreau

Only those who dare to fail greatly can ever achieve greatly.

Robert F. Kennedy

If you don't like something, change it.

Maya Angelou

You can do anything you wish to do, have anything you wish to have, be anything you wish to be.

Robert Collier

I can give you a six-word formula for success: Think things through – then follow through.

Edward Rickenbacker

Be yourself, who else is better qualified.

Frank J. Giblin, III

Trust yourself.

Foster C. McClellan

When in doubt, risk it.

Holbrook Jackson

Think for yourself and let others enjoy the privilege of doing so too.

Voltaire

Hold yourself responsible for a higher standard than anybody expects of you.

Henry Ward Beecher

Act as if it were impossible to fail.

Dorothea Brand

When placed in command – take charge.

Norman Schwarzkopf

Stop looking for your purpose – Be it.

Dr. Wayne Dyer

There is one thing stronger than all the world, and that is an idea whose time has come.

Victor Hugo

Accept the challenges, so that you may feel the exhilaration of victory.

General George Patton

You can have anything you want if you want it desperately enough.

Sheila Graham

Each of us can make a difference in the life of another.

George Bush

You are the only person on earth who can use your ability.

Zig Ziglar

Just do what you do best.

Red Auerbach

To play it safe is not to play.

Robert Altman

Every man believes that he has a greater possibility.

Ralph Waldo Emerson

If you don't like the way the world is, you change it.

Marian Wright Edelman

We must be the change we wish to see in the world.

Mahatma Gandhi

Chapter 7 – Getting Started

A good plan executed right now is better than a perfect plan executed next week.

George S. Patton

A journey of a thousand miles must begin with a single step.

Chinese Proverb

The way to escape your problem is to solve it.

Robert Anthony

Apparently there is nothing that cannot happen today.

Mark Twain

The beginning is the most important part of the work.

Plato

Whatever you can do, or dream you can, begin it.

Johann Wolfgang von Goethe

To climb steep hills require slow place at first.

William Shakespeare

Mighty rivers can easily be leaped at their source.

Publilius Syrus

The first and most important step towards success is the feeling that we can succeed.

Nelson Boswell

If we wait for the moment when everything, absolutely everything is ready, we shall never begin.

Ivan Turegeneu

You don't have to see the whole staircase, just take the first step.

Martin Luther King, Jr.

There are risks and cost to a program of action, but they are far less than the long-range risk and cost of comfortable inaction.

John F. Kennedy.

It is easier to keep up than to catch up.

Leo D. Bardsley

You never stub your toe standing still.

Charles F. Kettering

You cannot build a reputation on what you intend to do.

Liz Smith

Action is the antidote to despair.

Joan Baez

Arriving at one goal is the starting point to another.

John Dewey

If you wish to reach the highest, begin at the lowest.

Publius Syrus

Before everything else, getting ready is the secret to success.

Henry Ford

What the wise do in the beginning, fools do in the end.

Warren Buffet

All great things began on a day much like this one.

Morgan Rodgers

To begin with, you must know what you want.

Mary Kay Ash

Everyone who got where he is had to begin where he was.

Richard L. Evans

In creating, the only hard thing to do is begin; a grass blade is no easier to make than an oak.

James Russell Lowell

The indispensable first step to getting the things you want out of life is this: decide what you want.

Ben Stein

There is no such thing as a long piece of work, except one that you dare not start.

Charles Baudelaire

All glory comes from daring to begin.

Eugene F. Ware

You won't win if you don't begin.

Robert Schuler

Never leave that till tomorrow which you can do today.

Benjamin Franklin

With the possible exception of the equator, everything begins somewhere.

Peter Robert Fleming

Let us watch well our beginning, and results will manage themselves.

Alexander Clark

How wonderful it is that nobody need wait a single moment before starting to improve the world.

Anne Frank

A major part of successful living lies in the ability to put first things first.

Robert J. McKain

I take a simple view of life: Keep your eyes open and get on with it.

Sir Lawrence Oliver

You can either take action or you can hang back and hope for a miracle.

Peter F. Drucker

The great end of life is not knowledge but action.

Thomas Henry Huxley

You must get involved to have an impact.

John H. Holcomb

If you wait, all that happens is that you get older.

Larry McMurtry

The secret to getting ahead is getting started.

Sally Berger

Start by doing what's necessary, then what's possible, and suddenly you are doing the impossible.

St. Francis of Assisi

Nobody can do it for you.

Ralph Cordiner

A man who removes a mountain begins by carrying away small stones.

William Faulkner

Sometimes you just have to take the leap and build your wings on the way down.

Kobi Yamada

Indecision is often worst than wrong action.

Gerald Ford

If you put off everything till you're sure of it, you'll never get nothing done.

Norman Vincent Peale

Action will remove the doubts that theory cannot solve.

Tehyi Hsieh

Twenty years from now you will be disappointed by things you didn't do more than the ones you did do.

Mark Twain

Searching is half the fun; life is much more manageable when thought of as a scavenger hunt as opposed to a surprise party.

Jimmy Buffet

When it comes to getting things done, we need fewer architects and more brick layers.

Colleen C. Barret

Chapter 8 – Leadership

Leadership is an action, not a word.

Richard Cooley

You cannot train a horse with shouts and expect it to obey a whisper.

Pagobert P. River

Never claim as a right what you can ask as a favor.

William Lyon Phelps

The leader must know, must know that he knows and must be able to make it abundantly clear to those about him that he knows.

Clarence B. Randall

If you don't know where you are going, you will probably end up somewhere else.

Laurence J. Peter

Anger manages everything badly.

Statius

Once a decision was made, I did not worry about it afterward.

Harry S. Truman

Leadership is action, not position.

Donald H. McGannon

No person can be a good leader unless he takes a genuine joy in the successes of those under him.

W. H. Nance

The person who knows how is ever destined to work for the person who knows why.

Richard Moorehead

You don't become a leader because you say you are. It's much more what you do than what you say.

Sparky Anderson

Anyone can steer the ship when the sea is calm.

Publilius Syrus

The shepherd always tries to persuade the sheep that their interest and his own are the same.

Stendhal

Lead, follow, or get the hell out of the way.

Ted Turner

The only safe ship in a storm is leadership.

Faye Wattleton

The best executive is the one who has sense enough to pick good men to do what he wants done, and self-restraint enough to keep from meddling with them while they do it.

Theodore Roosevelt

A leader is one who knows the way, goes the way, and shows the way.

John C. Maxwell

We herd sheep, we drive cattle, we lead people.

George S. Patton

If you're not one step ahead of the crowd, you'll soon be a step behind everyone else.

Tom Landry

I am more afraid of an army of 100 sheep led by a lion than an army of 100 lions lead by a sheep.

Tallerand

Truly great leaders spend as much time collecting and acting on feedback as they do providing it.

Alexander Lucia

People are more easily led than driven.

David Harold Fink

The view only changes for the lead dog.

Sergeant Preston of the Yukon

You do not lead by hitting people over the head – that's assault not leadership.

Dwight d. Eisenhower

How far would Moses have gone if he had taken a poll in Egypt?

Harry Truman

No man will make a great leader who wants to do it all himself, or to get all the credit for doing it.

Andrew Carnegie

Part of being a good leader is knowing who to follow.

Andrew Rodriguez

It is not fair to ask of others what you are not willing to do yourself.

Eleanor Roosevelt

Management is doing things right; leadership is doing the right thing.

Peter Drucker

Good management is the art of making problems so interesting and their solutions so constructive that everyone wants to work and deal with them.

Paul Hawken

A leader is someone who steps back from the entire system and tries to build a more collaborative, more innovative system that will work over the long term.

Robert Reich

'Tis skill not strength that governs a ship.

Thomas Fuller

A leader is a dealer in hope.

Napoleon Bonaparte

A sense of humor is part of the art of leadership, of getting along with people, of getting things done.

Dwight D. Eisenhower

A chief is a man who assumes responsibility.

Anoine de Saint-Exupery

Management by objectives works if you first think through your objectives.

Peter Drucker

Good management consists of showing average people how to do the work of superior people.

John D Rockefeller

My basic principle is that you don't make decisions because they are easy; you don't make them because they are deep; you don't make them because they're popular; you make them because they're right.

Theodore Hesburgh

Leadership is the capacity to translate vision into reality.

Warren G. Bennis

Be willing to make decisions.

T. Boone Pickens

The buck stops with the guy who signs the checks.

Robert Murdoch

Leadership is practical not so much in words as in attitude and in actions.

Harold S. Green

Leadership should be born out of the understanding of the needs of those who would be affected by it.

Marian Anderson

Good leaders are like baseball umpires; they go practically unnoticed when doing their jobs right.

Byrd Baggett

Good leaders make people feel that they're at the very heart of things, not at the periphery.

Warren Bennis

Effective leadership is putting first things first.

Stephen Covey

In the simplest of terms, a leader is one who knows where he wants to go, and gets up and goes.

John Erksine

The very essence of leadership is that you have to have a vision.

Theodore Hesburgh

The difference between a boss and a leader: a boss says, "Go" – a leader says, "Let's go".

E. M. Kelly

Leadership is a combination of strategy and character.

General H. Norman Schwarzkopf

A good leader is a person who takes a little more than his share of the blame and a little less share of the credit.

John C. Maxwell

Leadership is influence.

John C. Maxwell

Leaders are visionaries with a poorly developed sense of fear and no concept of the odds against them.

Dr. Robert Jarvik

Leadership, like swimming, cannot be learned by reading about it.

Henry Mintzberg

Inventory can be managed; people must be led – by example.

Ross Perot

You must have both vision and a capacity to implement it.

Shimon Peres

Whatever your position in your organization, you can and should lead.

Donald H. Weiss

It is time for a new generation of leadership, to cope with new problems and new opportunities.

John F. Kennedy

Indeed, a prerequisite of being a leader boils down to the fact that people see you as one.

Donald H. Weiss

The question, "Who ought to be boss:" is like asking "Who ought to be the tenor in the quartet?" (Obviously, the man who can sing tenor.)

Henry Ford

The art of conversation is the language of leadership.

James Humes

There are no office hours for leaders.

Cardinal J. Gibbons

The speed of the leader determines the rate of the pack.

Wayne Lukas

The challenge of leadership is to be strong, but not rude; be kind, but not weak; be bold, but not bully; be thoughtful, but not lazy; be humble, but not timid; be proud, but not arrogant; have humor, but without folly.

Jim Rohn

People buy into the leader before they buy into their vision.

John C. Maxwell

Pull the string, and it will follow wherever you wish. Push it and it will go nowhere at all.

Dwight D. Eisenhower

As a manager the important thing is not what happens when you are there, but what happens when you are not there.

Ken Blanchard

Surround yourself with the best people you can find, delegate authority, and don't interfere.

Ronald Reagan

Leaders get out in front and stay there by raising the standards by which they judge themselves – and by which they are willing to be judged.

Frederick Smith

Leadership and learning are indispensable to each other.

John F. Kennedy

Happiness: the full use of your powers along lines of excellence.

John F. Kennedy

The leader who expects his people to perform their best will achieve the greatest results.

Joe Batten

The ability to focus attention on important things is a defining characteristic of intelligence.

Robert Shiller

The ability to confront issues is really important to a successful career, maybe even a successful life.

Robert Shiller

Courage is contagious. When a brave man takes a stand, the spines of others are stiffened.

Reverend Billy Graham

The king is the man who can.

Thomas Carlyle

A true leader is easy to find – because even when they follow, they lead.

Katie Santo

The only real training for leadership is leadership.

Anthony Jay

If you lead the people with correctness, who will dare not to be correct.

Confucius

An army of deer led by a lion is more feared than an army of lions led by a deer.

Phillip II of Macedon

An executive is a man who decides; sometimes he decides right; but always he decides.

John H. Patterson

I learned that a great leader is a man who has the ability to get other people to do what they don't like to do and like it.

Harry Truman

Leaders don't create followers; they create more leaders.

Tom Peters

The executive exists to make sensible exceptions to general rules.

Elting E. Morison

Effective leaders are not preachers; they are doers.

Peter Drucker

Lots of folks confuse bad management with destiny.

Ken Hubbard

The price of greatness is responsibility.

Winston Churchill

Leadership is the art of getting someone else to do something you want done because he wants to do it.

Dwight D. Eisenhower

One of the test of leadership is the ability to recognize a problem before it becomes an emergency.

Arnold Glasgow

Leaders get their authority from those they lead.

Michael H. Popkin

It's not much use being a leader if no one is willing to follow you.

Michael H. Popkin

Making decisions is what leaders are paid for.

Joe. D. Batten

Chapter 9 – Motivation

There is no such thing in anyone's life as an unimportant day.

Alexander Wolcott

Yesterday is a cancelled check; tomorrow is a promissory note; today is ready cash – use it.

Kay Lyons

Progress is not created by contented people.

Frank Tygen

Even if you're on the right track, you'll get run over if you just sit there.

Will Rogers

There are no hopeless situations; there are only people who have grown hopeless about them.

Clare Booth Luce

Do what you love, love what you do, and deliver more than you promise.

Harvey Mackay

The only place where success comes before work is in a dictionary.

Vidal Sassoon

You will only be remembered for two things: the problems you solve or the ones you create.

Mike Murdock

I like the dreams of the future better than the history of the past.

Thomas Jefferson

Do what you can, with what you have, where you are.

Theodore Roosevelt

Swing hard, in case they throw the ball where you're swinging.

Duke Snider

Everybody has sixty seconds to a minute, sixty minutes to an hour, twenty-four hours to a day; the difference is what we do with that time and how we use it.

Lou Holtz

There is much more opportunity than there are people to see it.

Thomas Edison

Some people see things as they are and say why. I dream of things that never were and say why not.

Robert F. Kennedy

The quality of a person's life is in direct proportion to their commitment to excellence, regardless of their chosen field of endeavor.

Vincent T. Lombardi

It's kind of fun to do the impossible.

Walt Disney

Everything comes to him who hustles while he waits.

Thomas Edison

It is not because things are difficult that we do not dare, it is because we do not dare that things are difficult.

Seneca

The roots of true achievement lie in the will to become the best that you can become.

Harold Taylor

We must be the change we wish to see in the world.

Mahatma Gandhi

Anything you can do needs to be done, so pick up the tool of your choice and get started.

Ben Linder

Set your goals high and don't stop till you get there.

Bo Jackson

Work as though you would live forever, and live as though you would die today.

Ogmandino

First say to yourself what you would be; then do what you have to do.

Epictetus

To succeed – you need something to hold on to, something to motivate you, something to inspire you.

Tony Dorsett

Undertake something that is difficult; it will do you good.

Ronald E. Osborn

If you want creative workers, give them enough time to play.

John Cleese

The winds and the waves are always on the side of the ablest navigators.

Edward Gibbon

Twenty years from now you will be more disappointed by the things that you didn't do than by the ones you did do.

Mark Twain

Do the uncommon things of life in an uncommon way.

George Washington Carver

For many are called, but few are chosen.

Matthew 22:14

Only those who dare to fail greatly can ever achieve greatly.

Robert F. Kennedy

Hold yourself responsible for a higher standard than anybody expects of you.

Henry Ward Beecher

Do all the good you can, by all the means you can, in all the ways you can, in all the places you can, at all the times you can, to all the people you can, as long as ever you can.

John Wesley

There are many ways of going forward, but only one way of standing still.

Franklin D. Roosevelt

Well done is better than well said.

Ben Franklin

Go confidently in the direction of your dreams.

Henry David Thoreau

Live the life you have imagined.

Henry David Thoreau

It is never too late to be what you might have been.

George Eliot

It's only competition if you are losing.

Morgan Rodgers

While it is important to win, it's imperative to compete.

Dave Weinbaum

Sometimes you must do the thing you cannot do.

Eleanor Roosevelt

Greatness is not in where we stand, but in what direction we are moving.

Oliver Wendell Holmes

Don't let life discourage you; everyone who got where he is had to begin where he was.

Richard L. Evans

If no one ever took risks, Michelangelo would have painted the Sistine floor.

Neil Simon

There isn't a person anywhere that isn't capable of doing more than he thinks he can.

Henry Ford

If you really want something, you can figure out how to make it happen.

Cher

The world is not good enough – we must make it better.

Alice Walker

Temporary failure is merely an opportunity to more intelligently begin again.

Henry Ford

To be a success in business, be daring, be first, be different.

Marchant

No matter how good things are, you can always improve, always improve, always improve.

Ross Perot

You play the hand you're dealt.

Christopher Reeve

We will either find a way or make one.

Hannibal

Make the most of yourself by fanning the tiny inner sparks of possibility into flames of achievement.

Foster C. McClellan

The will to win, the desire to succeed, the urge to reach your full potential – these are the keys that will unlock the door to personal excellence.

Eddie Robinson

To get what you want, stop doing what isn't working.

Dennis Weaver

It is difficult to steer a parked car, so get moving.

Henrietta Mears

The ultimate goal should be doing your best and enjoying it.

Peggy Fleming

If I didn't believe the answer could be found, I wouldn't be working on it.

Dr. Florence Sabin

Hard work is the key to success, so work diligently on any project you undertake.

Charles Lazarus

Making a success of the job at hand is the best step toward the kind you want.

Bernard M. Barach

Fight the tendency to quit while you're behind.

Dave Weinbaum

My philosophy is that not only are you responsible for your life, but doing the best at this moment puts you in the best place for the next moment.

Ophra Winfrey

Dream big, plan well, work hard, smile always and good things will happen.

Sally Huss

We all have the capacity to be great.

Peter Koestenbaum

Facing it – always facing it – that's the way to get through.

Joseph Conrad

The people who get on in this world are the people who get up and look for the circumstances they want, and if they can't find them, make them.

George Bernard Shaw

Freedom to be your best means nothing unless you're willing to do your best.

Colon Powell

Determine that the thing can and shall be done, and then we shall find the way.

Abraham Lincoln

A man who wants to do something will find a way; a man who doesn't will find an excuse.

Stephen Dolley, Jr.

I believe that the very purpose of our life is to seek happiness.

Dalai Lama

Act energetic and positive even when you don't feel like it.

Jenny E. Beeh

You may get skinned knees and elbows, but it's worth it if you score a spectacular goal.

Mia Hamm

Whenever you see a successful business, someone once made a courageous decision.

Peter Drucker

If you accept the expectations of others, especially negatives ones, then you never will change the outcome.

Michael Jordan

I do the very best I know how; the very best I can; and I mean to keep on doing so until the end.

Abraham Lincoln

Winners are those people who make a habit of doing the things losers are uncomfortable doing.

Ed Foreman

The elevator to success is out of order; use the stairs.

Joe Girard

If you can imagine it, you can achieve it. If you can dream it, you can become it.

Keith D. Harrell

Chapter 10 – Pat on the Back

Spoken from the heart almost any word will do.

Bill Walton

Patting a fellow on the back is the best way to get a chip off his shoulder.

Mary H. Waldrip

The best thing to do behind a friend's back is pat it.

Ruth Brillhart

If a man does his best, what else is there?

George S. Patton

I can live for two months on a good compliment.

Mark Twain

A hero is a man who does what he can.

Roman Rolland

You spend an evening with some people; with others you invest it.

Evan Esar

Praise is like sunshine to the human spirit; we cannot flower and grow without it.

Jess Lair

Words of encouragement fan the spark of genius into the flame of achievement.

Wilfred A. Peterson

Get someone else to blow your horn and the sound will carry twice as far.

Will Rogers

Correction does much, but encouragement does more.

Goethe

The finest gift you can give someone is encouragement.

Sidney Madwed

The sweetest of all sounds is praise.

Xenophon

The credit belongs to those people who are actually in the arena.

Theodore Roosevelt

The best way to cheer yourself up is to try to cheer somebody else up.

Mark Twain

Never lose a chance of saying a kind word.

William Makepeace Thackeray

It is up to us to give ourselves recognition.

Bernard Berkowitz

Most of us, swimming against the tides of trouble the world knows nothing about, need only a bit of praise or encouragement – and we will make the goal.

Jerome D. Fleisman

One of the sanest, surest, and most generous joys of life comes from being happy over the good fortune of others.

Archibald Rutledge

Tell a person they are brave and you help them become so.

Thomas Carlyle

If you would lift me up you must be on higher ground.

Ralph Waldo Emerson

I am always longing to be with men more excellent than myself.

Charles Lamb

Brains, like hearts, go where they are appreciated.

Robert S. McNamara

A pat on the back, though only a few vertebrae remove from a kick in the pants, is miles ahead in results.

Bennett Cerf

Gratitude unlocks the fullness of life.

Melody Beattie

There are two things people want more than sex and money – recognition and praise.

Mary Kay Ash

Few things help an individual more than to place responsibility upon him and to let him know that you trust him.

Booker T. Washington

Swift gratitude is the sweetest.

Greek Proverb

I have yet to be bored by someone paying me a compliment.

Otto Van Isch

Praise can be your most valuable asset as long as you don't aim it at yourself.

O.A. Battista

Kind words do not cost much – yet they accomplish much.

Blaise Pasca

If you can't get a compliment any other way, pay yourself one.

Mark Twain

Praise, like gold and diamonds, owes its value only to its scarcity.

Samuel Johnson

Remember that a person's name is to that person the sweetest and most important sound in any language.

Dale Carnegie

Each of us can make a difference in the life of another.

George Bush

Encouragement is oxygen to the soul.

George M. Adams

Chapter 11 – Team Work

Drive as if you owned the other car.

Hugh Allen

You spend an evening with some people, with others you invest it.

Evan Esar

A man only learns by two things; one is reading and the other is association with smarter people.

Will Rogers

If you cannot win, make the one ahead of you break the record.

Jan McKeithen

We can't all be heroes. Somebody has to sit on the curb and clap as they go by.

Will Rogers

The nice thing about teamwork is that you always have others on your side.

Margaret Carty

Light is the task when many share the load.

Homer

No one is useless in the world who lightens the burden of another.

Charles Dickens

When we turn to one another for counsel, we reduce the number of our enemies.

Kahlil Gibran

None of us is as smart as all of us.

Peter B. Grazier

Do what is right, do the best you can and treat others like you want to be treated.

Lou Holtz

A community is like a ship, everyone ought to be prepared to take the helm.

Henrik Ibsen

A dwarf standing on the shoulders of a giant may see further than a giant himself.

Robert Burton

We must learn to live together as brothers or perish together as fools.

Martin Luther King, Jr.

We're all on this boat together, but some of us aren't rowing hard enough.

Moby in the Morning

The quality of an organization can never exceed the quality of the minds that make it up.

Harold R. McAlinda

Words divide us, action unites us.

Slogan of the Tupamaros

It is amazing what you can accomplish if you do not care who gets the credit.

Harry S. Truman

The way a team plays as a whole determines its success.

Babe Ruth

Socializing is a key element of the creative process.

Walt Disney

The greater the loyalty of a group toward the group, the greater the motivation among the members to achieve the goals of the group, and the greater the probability that the group will achieve its goal.

Rensis Likert

A candle loses nothing by lighting another candle.

Father James Keller

Everyone ought to be prepared to take the helm.

Henrik Ibsen

When we seek to discover the best in others, we somehow bring out the best in ourselves.

William Arthur Ward

It's easy to get good players. Getting 'em to play together, that's the hard part.

Casey Stengel

Thousands of candles can be lighted from a single candle, and the life of the candle will not be shortened.

Buddha

There is something more powerful than anybody – and that is everybody.

Captain Eddy Rickenbacker

Never doubt that a small group of thoughtful committed citizens can change the world. Indeed, it is the only thing that ever has.

Margaret Mead

You get the best out of others when you give the best of yourself.

Harry Firestone

The important thing to recognize is that it takes a team, and the team ought to get credit for the wins and the loses.

Philip Caldwell

Now is the time to recognize that which unites us is greater than that which divides us.

Al Gore

No man is an island, entire of itself; every man is a piece of the continent.

John Donne

The question is usually not how well each person works, but how well they work together.

Vince Lombardi

You don't get harmony when everybody sings the same note.

Doug Floyd

The secret to success is to work less as individuals and more as a team.

Knute Rockne

If you don't invest very much, then defeat doesn't hurt very much and winning is not very exciting.

Dick Vermeil

Great discoveries and achievements invariably involve the cooperation of many minds.

Alexander Graham Bell

If I advance, follow me. If I stop, push me. If I fall, inspire me.

Robert Cushing

The most important single ingredient in the formula of success is knowing how to get along with people.

Theodore Roosevelt

The valuable person in business is the individual who can and will cooperate with others.

Donald H. Weiss

We will either find a way, or make one.

Hannibal

Each of us brings to our job, whatever it is, our lifetime of experience and our values.

Sandra Day O'Connor

Cooperation is the thorough conviction that nobody can get there unless everybody gets there.

Virginia Burden

Our prime purpose in this life is to help others.

The Dalai Lama

The strengths of an organization can be no stronger than the strengths of the personal relationships, the quality of the minds, and the strengths of the shared values within it.

Joe Batten

Whether called "task forces", "quality circles", "problem solving groups", or "shared responsibility teams", such vehicles for greater participation at all levels are an important part of an innovating company.

Rosabeth Moss Kanter

Coming together is a beginning; keeping together is progress; working together is success.

Henry Ford

When you build bridges you can keep crossing them.

Rick Pitino

We need a spirit of community, a sense that we are all in this together.

Bill Clinton

The same fence that shuts others out shuts you in.

Bill Copeland

I use not only all the brains I have, but all I can borrow.

Woodrow Wilson

What do we live for if it is not to make life less difficult for each other?

George Eliot

You can't help someone get up a hill without getting closer to the top yourself.

General H. Norman Schwarzkopf

I have always thought the greatest symbol of common sense was building a bridge.

Franklin D. Roosevelt

We get things done when we get into relationships with people of similar goals and aspirations.

Margie Keith-Cooper

We get the best out of others when we give the best of ourself.

Harry Firestone

We cannot hold a torch to light another's path without brightening our own.

Ben Sweetland

If we would just support each other – that's ninety percent of the problem.

Edward Gardner

What concerns everyone can only be resolved by everyone.

Friedrich Durrenmatt

In order for me to look good, everybody around me has to look good.

Doris Drury

Only the guy who isn't rowing has time to rock the boat.

Saunders

If you want creative workers, give them enough time to play.

John Cleese

There's a delight that comes with helping other people.

Paul Newman

It is one of the most beautiful compensations of life that no man can sincerely try to help another without helping himself.

Ralph Waldo Emerson

People seldom improve when they have no other model but themselves to copy after.

Gold Smith

Cooperation isn't the absence of conflict but a means of managing conflict.

Deborah Tannen

Never give up on anybody.

Hubert H. Humphrey

Made in the USA
Charleston, SC
08 April 2010